I0411222

Manage Finances with QuickBooks Online

Master Your Money: A Step-by-Step Guide to
Conquering QuickBooks Online as a Beginner. Take
Charge of Your Financial Future, The Essential Guide to
Managing Your Finances with QuickBooks Online

By

Clara Higgins

Copyright notice!!!

Copyright © 2024 Clara Higgins. All Rights Reserved.

This book, article, artwork, content and its contents are the intellectual property of Clara Higgins. The legal rights to this work are safeguarded by copyright laws and international agreements.

All rights are reserved. Without obtaining the written consent of the copyright owner, it is prohibited to reproduce, distribute, or transmit any portion of this book, article, artwork, content through various means such as photocopying, recording, or electronic methods. However, there are exceptions for limited quotations incorporated in critical reviews and specific noncommercial uses authorized by copyright law.

Any unauthorized use, reproduction, or distribution of this book, article, artwork, content without the express permission of Clara Higgins is strictly prohibited and may result in legal action.

Table of Contents

INTRODUCTION

Ditch the Spreadsheets, Embrace the Future: Introducing Manage Finances with QuickBooks Online

Do you ever glance at your overflowing inbox, your bulging shoebox of receipts, and your ever-growing spreadsheet with a sinking feeling? Does the mere thought of "finances" trigger a cold sweat and dreams of runaway spreadsheets? Fear not, weary warrior, for **Manage Finances with QuickBooks Online** is your cavalry, charging in to banish financial chaos and usher in an era of clarity and control.

This isn't just another dusty accounting manual; it's your financial liberation manifesto. No more wrestling with cryptic formulas or deciphering ancient check stubs. QuickBooks Online, your trusty digital companion, is here to streamline your finances, automate the tedious, and illuminate the path to financial freedom.

Whether you're a business owner yearning for peace of mind, a freelancer craving invoice mastery, or an everyday hero wrestling with household budgets, **Manage Finances with QuickBooks Online** equips you with the tools and knowledge to:

- **Transform your shoebox into a symphony:** Ditch the paper avalanche and import your transactions with ease. Say goodbye to shoebox shuffles and hello to organized data with the power to tell the story of your finances.

- **Become an invoice ninja:** Craft professional invoices in seconds, track payments like a hawk, and ditch the overdue dance forever. Your clients will sing your praises, and your bank account will thank you.

- **Budget like a boss:** Say goodbye to guesswork and hello to data-driven budgeting. Set realistic goals, track your progress, and adjust with confidence. No more "mystery money" disappearing – every penny has a purpose.

- **Tax time tranquility:** Breathe easy when tax season rolls around. Generate accurate reports, categorize expenses seamlessly, and face the IRS with a Zen-like calm. QuickBooks Online simplifies your tax life, leaving you free to focus on what you do best.

- **Unleash the power of insights:** Get a bird's-eye view of your finances with intuitive dashboards and comprehensive reports. Spot trends, identify opportunities, and make informed decisions based on actual data, not gut feelings.

Forget spreadsheets and shoeboxes. This is the future of finance. Forget clunky software and jargon-filled manuals. **Manage Finances with QuickBooks Online** is written in your language, with step-by-step instructions, real-world examples, and a healthy dose of humor to keep you motivated.

Join the thousands who have traded spreadsheet purgatory for QuickBooks Online paradise. This book is your passport to financial clarity, control, and (dare we say) enjoyment.

So, open your mind, open this book, and open the door to a world where your finances work for you, not the other way around. It's time to ditch the chaos and embrace the future with **Manage Finances with QuickBooks Online.** Your financial freedom awaits!

Chapter 1

Foundational Steps to Financial Freedom

Goodbye Chaos, Hello QuickBooks Online: Your Portal to Financial Nirvana

Do you wake up in a cold sweat, your heart pounding at the mere thought of "finances"? Is your desk a graveyard of receipts, your inbox a tsunami of bank statements, and your spreadsheet skills...well, let's just say Excel doesn't sing your praises. Fear not, weary warrior of the financial jungle, for QuickBooks Online is your cavalry, charging in to banish the chaos and usher in an era of clarity and control.

Forget clunky software and jargon-filled manuals. QuickBooks Online is the financial fairy godmother who waves her digital wand and transforms your shoebox of receipts into a symphony of organized data. No more deciphering ancient check stubs or wrestling with cryptic formulas. This isn't just another accounting manual; it's your financial liberation manifesto, your escape hatch from the spreadsheet purgatory.

Imagine a world where:

- **Transactions dance in perfect order:** Import your data with ease, categorize expenses like a ninja, and watch your financial history unfold in a beautifully organized ballet. No more shoebox shuffles, just a well-choreographed digital record of every penny.

- **Invoices become your superpower:** Craft professional invoices in seconds, track payments like a hawk, and banish overdue notices to the realm of forgotten nightmares. Your clients will shower you with gold stars, and your bank account will sing a joyful chorus.

- **Budgets blossom with intention:** Ditch the guesswork and embrace data-driven budgeting. Set realistic goals, track your progress with laser focus, and adjust your spending with the confidence of a financial sensei. No more "mystery money" disappearing; every penny finds its purpose.

- **Tax season transforms from monster to mini-vacation:** Breathe easy when April rolls around. Generate accurate reports, categorize expenses seamlessly, and face the IRS with the Zen-like calm of a financial rockstar.

QuickBooks Online simplifies your tax life, leaving you free to spend that time making memories, not battling bureaucracy.

- **Insights become your guiding light:** Get a bird's-eye view of your finances with intuitive dashboards and comprehensive reports. Spot trends, identify opportunities, and make informed decisions based on actual data, not gut feelings. No more flying blind; you'll be navigating the financial landscape like a seasoned captain.

QuickBooks Online isn't just software; it's a financial revolution disguised as a friendly digital companion. It's written in your language, with step-by-step instructions, real-world examples, and a healthy dose of humor to keep you motivated. Join the thousands who have traded spreadsheet purgatory for QuickBooks Online paradise. This book is your passport to financial clarity, control, and (dare we say) enjoyment.

So, open your mind, open this book, and open the door to a world where your finances work for you, not the other way around. It's time to ditch the chaos and hello QuickBooks Online. Your financial freedom awaits, ready to blossom under the nurturing guidance of this digital oasis.

Let's embark on this journey together, shall we?
Welcome to the future of finance, where the only
spreadsheets you'll encounter are the ones you choose to
create, overflowing with the sweet data of your financial
success story.

Chapter 2

Setting Up for Success: Building Your Financial Fortress with QuickBooks Online

The thrill of a fresh start isn't just reserved for New Year's resolutions. With QuickBooks Online, you can experience that invigorating "blank slate" feeling any time you choose. No more dusty shoeboxes piled high, no more cryptic spreadsheets singing the blues. Here, in this digital domain, you have the opportunity to build your very own financial fortress, a citadel of clarity and control. But before you hoist the flag of financial freedom, there's a crucial first step: **Setting up your account and connecting your bank.**

Think of it as laying the foundation of your financial empire. It might seem daunting at first, like navigating uncharted territory, but fear not, intrepid explorer! This chapter will be your trusty map, guiding you through the process with clear instructions and a healthy dose of encouragement.

Step 1: Planting the Seed - Creating Your Account

First things first, let's plant the seed of your financial future. Head over to QuickBooks Online and click on the "Sign Up" button. Don't worry, commitment-phobes, you can try it free for 30 days – plenty of time to fall in love with the streamlined organization and control this platform offers.

Once you've filled in your basic information, choose your plan. Remember, a financial fortress needs strong walls, so pick the one that best suits your needs. Whether you're a solopreneur building your empire brick by brick or a small business ready to scale the financial Everest, there's a plan tailor-made for you.

Step 2: Building the Bridge - Connecting Your Bank

Now, for the crucial step: connecting your bank. This might sound intimidating, but QuickBooks Online makes it as smooth as butter gliding across a hot pan. Simply select your bank from the extensive list – chances are, it's there – and follow the on-screen instructions. No need for manual data entry, no tedious bank visits – just a few clicks and you're in business.

Suddenly, your dusty bank statements transform into vibrant streams of data flowing right into your QuickBooks Online dashboard. Transactions categorize themselves like magic, expenses line up in neat rows, and your financial picture snaps into focus. It's like watching a blurry landscape sharpen into a breathtaking vista, a revelation of clarity amidst the financial fog.

Step 3: Customizing Your Domain - Making it Your Own

But wait, there's more! Your financial fortress isn't just a fortress; it's your palace, your financial haven. QuickBooks Online lets you personalize your experience with custom settings and preferences. Choose your currency, set your chart of accounts, and adjust everything to reflect your unique financial ecosystem. No cookie-cutter solutions here, just bespoke financial management tailor-made for you.

Bonus Tip: The Power of Automation

Remember that magical bridge you built to your bank? Now, let's automate it! Set up recurring transactions for things like rent or payroll, schedule automatic downloads of your bank statements, and watch your financial world run on autopilot. Imagine – coffee in hand, watching your finances manage themselves like a well-oiled machine. Automation is your secret weapon, freeing you to focus on what truly matters – building your business, conquering your goals, and celebrating the liberation of financial clarity.

Setting up your account and connecting your bank is not just the first step; it's the starting pistol of your financial revolution. With each click, you lay another brick in the foundation of your fortress, one that will stand strong in the face of financial chaos. So, take a deep breath, open your QuickBooks Online account, and embark on this transformative journey. Your financial freedom awaits, just beyond the threshold of clarity and control.

Chapter 3

Navigating the Dashboard: Understanding the interface, accessing key features, and customizing your workspace.

Welcome to the cockpit of your financial spaceship, intrepid explorer! Here, within the sleek and intuitive dashboard of QuickBooks Online, lies the power to chart your course towards financial clarity and control. No more scrambling through spreadsheets or deciphering dusty bank statements. This is your command center, a haven of organized data and powerful tools at your fingertips.

But before you blast off on your financial odyssey, let's take a stroll through the interface and familiarize ourselves with the controls. Think of it as a pre-flight check, ensuring you're comfortable and confident before navigating the vast expanse of your finances.

Central Hub: The Overview Panel

Imagine a majestic mountain peak, a vantage point from which you can survey your entire financial landscape. That's the Overview Panel, sitting proudly at the heart of your QuickBooks Online dashboard. Here, you'll find a snapshot of your financial health, displayed in clear, bite-sized chunks of information. Your bank balances dance across the screen, income and expenses tango in neat charts, and key metrics like unpaid bills blink a friendly reminder. It's your financial pulse monitor, keeping you informed and in control.

Charting Your Course: Essential Navigation Tools

Now, let's explore the menu bar, your trusty map and compass. From "Customers" to "Reports," each click opens a portal to specific realms of your financial world. Send invoices like intergalactic missives from the "Sales" section, track expenses like cosmic dust in the "Expenses" tab, and generate insightful reports like detailed star charts from the "Reports" menu. Remember, each section is carefully labeled and intuitively designed, making navigating your finances feel like a smooth spacewalk, not a perilous deep-space expedition.

Personalizing Your Starship: Customizing Your Workspace

But hold on, this is your financial vessel, and personalization is key! QuickBooks Online lets you adjust the dashboard to your unique needs. Rearrange panels like customizable modules, prioritize the information you need most, and even add widgets like financial news or motivational quotes to keep your financial engine humming. Make your dashboard feel like a reflection of your own financial aspirations, a space that inspires and empowers you to conquer your financial goals.

Bonus Tip: Embracing the Help Button – Your Celestial Guide

Feeling lost in the vast expanse of your financial universe? Fear not, for the "Help" button is your friendly AI copilot, always ready to navigate you out of any financial black hole. Click it, type your query, and watch as relevant articles, tutorials, and even step-by-step guides materialize on your screen. It's like having a financial Yoda whispering wisdom in your ear, guiding you with patience and knowledge.

Remember, navigating the QuickBooks Online dashboard isn't just about learning features; it's about unlocking the potential of your data. Every click, every report, every customized panel brings you closer to financial clarity and control.

Chapter 4

Taming the Transaction Beast: Importing data, categorizing transactions, and maintaining an organized financial picture.

Ah, the Transaction Beast. It lurks in shoeboxes, roars in overflowing inboxes, and unleashes chaos upon spreadsheets. Its tentacles of receipts, bank statements, and cryptic online purchases threaten to devour your financial sanity. But fear not, brave warrior, for within the digital walls of QuickBooks Online lies the ultimate weapon: the Power of Categorization. With it, you can transform the Beast's unruly rampage into a symphony of organized data, a financial oasis where clarity reigns supreme.

Step 1: Importing the Beast – Embrace the Data Tsunami

First things first, we must face the Beast head-on. Import your bank statements, drag and drop those shoebox receipts (yes, scanning apps are your allies!), and unleash the digital flood of transactions. Don't worry, QuickBooks Online acts like a financial dam, capturing and organizing every penny with its automated magic. No more manual data entry, no more frantic scribbling on notes – just a few clicks and the Beast's data becomes your obedient servant.

Step 2: The Art of Taming – Unleashing the Categorization Power

Now, for the pièce de résistance: unleash the categorization power! Each transaction, once imported, begs to be assigned a label. Groceries? Rent? Coffee date with a friend? With QuickBooks Online's intuitive interface, categorizing feels like playing a satisfying game of financial Tetris. Drag and drop, select from pre-defined categories, or create your own – the power is in your hands.

But wait, there's more! Watch as categorized transactions dance across your screen, revealing patterns and insights. Identify where your money goes, track spending habits, and uncover hidden financial truths. Did that "miscellaneous" category suddenly reveal a coffee addiction? Knowledge is power, and with accurate categorization, you hold the key to financial wisdom.

Step 3: Maintaining the Oasis – Embracing Automation and Regular Check-Ups

Remember, taming the Transaction Beast is an ongoing journey. Set up recurring transactions for predictable expenses like rent or gym memberships, and watch them automatically fall into their designated categories. Schedule bank downloads to keep your financial data fresh, and treat yourself to regular check-ups – a quick glance at your categorized expenses can be a mini-vacation from financial stress.

Bonus Tip: Conquering the Credit Card Chaos – Your Secret Weapon

Does the mere mention of credit card statements send shivers down your spine? Fear not! QuickBooks Online has your back. Connect your credit cards, and watch as charges magically appear, pre-categorized and ready to be tamed. No more manual reconciliation, no more late-night battles with cryptic statements. Breathe easy, credit card warriors, your financial oasis awaits.

Taming the Transaction Beast is not just about organization; it's about reclaiming control of your finances. With QuickBooks Online, you transform chaos into clarity, data into insights, and the Beast into a docile companion. So, step into the arena, embrace the power of categorization, and create your own financial paradise. Remember, you hold the key to a world where every penny has a purpose, every expense tells a story, and financial freedom sings a sweet song. Go forth, brave warrior, and conquer the Transaction Beast!

Chapter 5

Mastering Money Management Essentials: Your Financial Jedi Training in QuickBooks Online

Ah, money management. It's the elusive force that separates financial padawans from financial Jedi Masters. But fear not, aspiring financial samurai, for within the digital walls of QuickBooks Online lies the ultimate training ground: a dojo of essential skills ready to hone your budget-fu and expense-sensing abilities.

Chapter 1: Invoice Powerplay – Bending Income to Your Will

No Jedi Master is complete without mastering the lightsaber of invoicing. In QuickBooks Online, crafting invoices is a breeze. From professional templates to automated reminders, you'll wield this tool like a financial katana, slashing away at overdue payments and leaving a trail of satisfied clients in your wake. Track payment statuses with laser focus, send friendly reminders with a click, and watch your bank account flourish under the power of the perfect invoice.

Chapter 2: Expense Tracking Ninja – Demystifying the Financial Force

Every Jedi needs to understand the ebb and flow of the financial Force. And what better way to do that than by mastering the art of expense tracking in QuickBooks Online? Categorize your purchases with lightning speed, identify spending patterns like a financial Yoda, and uncover hidden budgetary truths. Is that latte habit threatening your financial nirvana? Fear not, the power of categorization lets you see your spending habits with Jedi-level clarity, paving the way for informed financial decisions.

Chapter 3: Build a Budget You Love – Embracing the Balance of the Force

A budget is your financial lightsaber, deflecting unnecessary expenses and guiding you towards financial peace. But forget rigid spreadsheets and restrictive numbers. In QuickBooks Online, budget-building is a joyful act of creation. Set realistic goals, allocate funds with intention, and track your progress with laser focus. Watch as your spending aligns with your values, feel the balance of the financial Force flowing through you, and celebrate each milestone like a true financial Jedi.

Chapter 4: Banking Harmony – Flowing with the Financial Current

No Jedi Master can ignore the mighty bank statements. But with QuickBooks Online, reconciliation is no longer a battle with cryptic numbers. Watch as bank transactions automatically download and align with your expenses, leaving you free to focus on the greater good of your financial future. No more late-night battles, no more spreadsheets of doom – just a harmonious flow of data, revealing a clear picture of your financial reality.

Bonus Tip: Automation – Your Secret Financial Ally

Embrace the power of the Force, young padawan! Set up recurring transactions for rent, bills, or even weekly coffee runs. Schedule bank downloads, automate invoice reminders, and watch your finances manage themselves like a well-oiled droid. This is your lightsaber on autopilot, freeing you to explore the vast galaxy of financial possibilities.

Mastering money management with QuickBooks Online isn't just about learning software; it's about developing the financial skills of a Jedi Master. You'll learn to control your income, understand your expenses, and align your spending with your values. This is your journey to financial enlightenment, where every budget is a victory, every tracked expense a step closer to your financial nirvana.

Chapter 6

Invoice Power Play: Creating professional invoices, sending them with ease, and tracking payments like a pro.

Ah, the invoice. A seemingly simple document, yet it holds the power to transform you from a nervous freelancer to a Zen Invoicing Master. Fear not, weary warrior of the freelance frontier, for within the digital walls of QuickBooks Online lies the ultimate arsenal: **Invoice Power Play.** Here, you'll wield the tools and techniques to craft professional invoices that sing, send them with lightning-fast efficiency, and track payments like a financial hawk. Prepare to unleash your inner accounting Jedi, ready to conquer overdue notices and claim your rightful place as a master of billable hours.

Step 1: Forge Your Invoice Lightsaber - Customize & Conquer

Think of your invoice as your personalized lightsaber. In QuickBooks Online, you can customize it to perfection. Choose from sleek templates that scream professionalism, add your logo with pride, and tweak every detail to reflect your brand. No more generic, soul-crushing invoices – these will be works of art, ready to impress your clients and secure your financial future.

Step 2: Master the Force of Automation - One-Click Invoicing Nirvana

Embrace the power of the Force, young Jedi! Create recurring invoices for loyal clients in a flash, schedule automatic reminders to keep late payments at bay, and watch your workflow flow with Jedi-level efficiency. QuickBooks Online takes care of the mundane, leaving you free to focus on your craft and conquer your billable hours.

Step 3: Send with Precision - Aim, Click, Send, Conquer

With a single click, send your invoices soaring into the digital ether. Track their progress in real-time, watch as they open (cue the dramatic music!), and celebrate each delivered masterpiece. No more chasing clients or printing envelopes – these invoices are digital rocketships, fueled by QuickBooks Online and guided by your impeccable targeting skills.

Step 4: Payment Tracking Mastery - The Hawk Takes Flight

Payment notifications? Overdue alerts? Consider them your enemy's TIE fighters, easily dispatched with the laser focus of your payment tracking skills. QuickBooks Online keeps everything transparent, from initial payment whispers to the sweet symphony of a fully-paid invoice. Monitor timelines, send polite reminders like a benevolent financial Jedi, and bask in the glory of on-time payments.

Bonus Tip: The Art of Follow-Up - A Gentle Nudge, Not a Lightsaber Attack

Remember, even the most skilled Jedi Knight needs to negotiate. Craft polite, professional follow-up emails for those invoices lingering in the "pending" zone. QuickBooks Online even offers customizable templates, ensuring your communication is clear, concise, and effective. A gentle nudge, not a lightsaber attack – that's the way of the Invoice Power Play Master.

Mastering the art of invoicing in QuickBooks Online is not just about sending bills; it's about empowerment, efficiency, and control. You'll learn to craft invoices that impress, send them with ease, and track payments like a financial hawk. This is your journey to invoicing nirvana, where overdue notices are but a distant memory and your bank account sings a joyful chorus of paid-in-full.

Chapter 7

Expense Tracking Ninja: Categorizing expenses for accuracy, understanding tax implications, and identifying spending patterns.

Ah, expenses. They lurk in receipts, whisper in bank statements, and can morph into financial shadows that haunt even the bravest entrepreneurs. But fear not, weary warriors of the financial frontier, for within the digital walls of QuickBooks Online lies the ultimate defense: Expense Tracking Ninja. Here, you'll hone your skills in the ancient art of categorization, master the delicate dance of tax implications, and unveil the hidden truths within your spending patterns. Prepare to shed the cloak of financial confusion and emerge as a true Expense Tracking Ninja, ready to conquer chaos and claim your rightful place as a master of money management.

Step 1: The Art of Categorization – Weaving Order from Chaos

Think of your transactions as a jumble of colorful threads. In QuickBooks Online, you wield the brush of categorization, transforming that tangled mess into a beautiful tapestry of understanding. From "Coffee

Breaks" to "Marketing Magic," assign each expense its rightful label with lightning speed. No more cryptic "miscellaneous" entries – these categories will sing a song of financial clarity, revealing where your money flows and what truly fuels your business.

Step 2: Tax Fu Master – Unraveling the Mystery of Deductions

Taxes? Don't let the mere mention send shivers down your spine. With QuickBooks Online's tax magic, deductibles whisper their secrets and business expenses transform into financial allies. Mark business meals, track travel costs, and categorize purchases with tax optimization in mind. No more confusing forms or late-night scrambling – QuickBooks Online guides you through the tax labyrinth, leaving you free to focus on your business goals.

Bonus Tip: Embrace the Automation Force – Set & Forget

Remember, a true Ninja is efficient. Set up recurring transactions for predictable expenses like rent or subscriptions, and watch them automatically fall into their designated categories. Schedule bank downloads to keep your financial data fresh, and bask in the glory of streamlined expense tracking. Let QuickBooks Online handle the mundane, while you focus on the exciting art of conquering your business goals.

Step 3: The Patterns Emerge – The Light Dawns on Your Spending

As you categorize and track, patterns begin to emerge from the shadows. Identify spending habits with laser focus, discover hidden trends, and unveil insights that will shape your financial path. Did that "office supplies" category suddenly reveal a stationery addiction? Knowledge is power, and with accurate expense tracking, you hold the key to financial wisdom.

Step 4: Budgeting with Clarity – Guiding Your Financial Ship

With the power of expense tracking, budgeting becomes a strategic maneuver, not a guessing game. Allocate funds with intention, adjust based on real-time data, and watch your financial ship sail towards its destination. No more rigid spreadsheets or restrictive numbers – these budgets are dynamic vessels, guided by your newfound understanding of your financial ecosystem.

Bonus Tip: Embrace the Report Whisperer – Unlocking the Secrets of Data

Reports, once cryptic scrolls, become your allies in QuickBooks Online. Generate insightful reports with a click, dive deeper into specific categories, and uncover hidden truths within your data. No more financial black holes – these reports are illuminating beacons, guiding you towards informed decisions and financial mastery.

Mastering expense tracking in QuickBooks Online is not just about organizing receipts; it's about understanding your financial reality and empowering yourself to make informed decisions. You'll learn to categorize with precision, decipher tax implications like a pro, and identify spending patterns that inform your future. This is your journey to financial enlightenment, where every expense tells a story and every category is a stepping stone on your path to success.

Chapter 8

Build a Budget You Love: Setting realistic budgeting goals, allocating funds with intention, and tracking progress without the stress.

Budgeting. The B-word. It conjures images of deprivation, rigid spreadsheets, and the nagging feeling of living in a financial straitjacket. But fear not, weary warriors of the financial wasteland, for within the digital walls of QuickBooks Online lies a revolutionary truth: Budgets can be your best financial friend, not your bully. Here, you'll transform yourself from a budget-phobic novice to a Master Builder of Money Mountains, crafting budget plans you'll actually love.

Step 1: Laying the Foundation – Setting Realistic Goals

Forget pie-in-the-sky fantasies of overnight millionaire-dom. True budget builders start with realistic goals that inspire, not intimidate. Do you crave a dream vacation? Aim for a monthly savings target you can celebrate, not cry over. Want to ditch the debt dragon? Set achievable benchmarks that track your progress, not fuel your frustration. Remember, small steps lead to giant financial leaps, so focus on goals that fit your unique financial terrain.

Step 2: Bricks and Mortar – Allocating Funds with Intention

Think of your budget as a beautiful financial mosaic. In QuickBooks Online, you'll wield the spatula of allocation, distributing your hard-earned cash with intention and purpose. Categorize your expenses wisely, from "Rent Royale" to "Latte Love," and assign each category a budget share that reflects your priorities. No more living paycheck to paycheck – this is about taking control, ensuring each dollar serves a purpose and fuels your journey towards financial freedom.

Bonus Tip: Embrace the Automation Army – Set & Forget, Thrive & Celebrate

Remember, a happy builder knows the power of delegation. Set up recurring transfers to savings goals, schedule bill payments so you never miss a deadline, and watch your budget run on autopilot. QuickBooks Online becomes your loyal financial assistant, freeing you to focus on the joys of money management, not the mundane tasks.

Step 3: Tracking with Tranquility – Monitoring Progress without the Stress

Tracking your budget shouldn't feel like scaling Mount Debtmore. In QuickBooks Online, progress unfolds with the grace of a sunrise. Watch as your spending aligns with your allocated shares, celebrate milestones with virtual fireworks, and adjust your plan with gentle nudges, not panicked overhauls. No more spreadsheets of doom – these financial reports are your cheerleaders, urging you onwards with every green checkmark and positive statistic.

Step 4: Celebrate the Climb – Rewarding Yourself for Financial Fitness

Budgeting shouldn't feel like a punishment. Remember, achieving your financial goals is cause for celebration! Treat yourself to a small reward as you reach milestones, savor the accomplishment of sticking to your plan, and let the joy of financial progress fuel your motivation. A guilt-free latte here, a weekend getaway there – these are not detours, they're pit stops on your journey to financial nirvana.

Bonus Tip: Embrace the Flexibility Force – Adjust & Adapt for Unforeseen Adventures

Life happens. Cars break down, unexpected vacations beckon, and that dream concert ticket materializes. Don't panic! True budget builders adapt with grace. QuickBooks Online lets you adjust your plan on the fly, reallocate funds with ease, and keep your financial mountain climbing on track, even when life throws a curveball.

Building a budget you love in QuickBooks Online is not just about numbers; it's about transformation. You'll learn to set realistic goals, allocate funds with intention, and track your progress without the stress. This is your journey to financial empowerment, where every budgeted dollar sings a joyful chorus of freedom and control.

Chapter 9

Banking Harmony: Reconciling bank statements, avoiding errors, and ensuring your financial records are accurate.

Ah, bank statements. They arrive with the fanfare of trumpets, promising tales of financial conquests, but often morph into discordant jumbles of numbers, leaving you scratching your head like a conductor facing a cacophony. Fear not, intrepid explorer of the financial frontier, for within the digital walls of QuickBooks Online lies the path to Banking Harmony. Here, you'll transform those chaotic concertos into symphonic statements of financial clarity, mastering reconciliation like a financial maestro and ensuring your records sing the sweet song of accuracy.

Step 1: The Overture – Importing the Data Tsunami

First things first, face the music - import those bank statements! Drag and drop them into QuickBooks Online, watch as transactions flood in like eager instruments, and prepare to conduct them into order. Don't worry, QuickBooks Online acts as your digital oboe, smoothing out the data flow and transforming the chaos into a manageable ensemble. No more manual entry madness – this is a one-click symphony you can conduct from the comfort of your virtual armchair.

Step 2: The Harmony of Categorization – Finding Each Note its Place

Now, for the true magic. Each transaction, a musical note, begs to be assigned its place in the financial orchestra. Groceries? Rent? A spontaneous karaoke night with friends? With QuickBooks Online's intuitive interface, categorization feels like playing a financial game of "Simon Says." Drag and drop, select from pre-defined categories, or create your own – the power is in your hands, maestro! Watch as categorized transactions dance across your screen, revealing patterns and insights like unexpected key changes. Did that "miscellaneous" section suddenly reveal a coffee addiction? Knowledge is power, and with accurate categorization, you hold the baton to financial wisdom.

Step 3: Reconciliation Riff – Detecting the Discordant Notes

No maestro worth their salt ignores the occasional off-key note. Reconciliation is your chance to identify discrepancies and harmonize your financial records.

Watch as bank transactions automatically align with your expenses, leaving you free to focus on the bigger picture. No more late-night battles with cryptic numbers, no more spreadsheets of doom – just a harmonious flow of data, revealing a clear picture of your financial reality.

Bonus Tip: Automation Harmony – Your Digital Sidekick

Embrace the power of the digital age! Set up recurring transactions for predictable expenses like rent or gym memberships, and watch them automatically fall into their designated categories. Schedule bank downloads to keep your financial data fresh, and treat yourself to regular check-ups – a quick glance at your categorized expenses can be a mini-vacation from financial stress.

Step 4: The Grand Finale – Celebrate the Financial Encore!

Reconciliation complete, your records sing in perfect harmony! Bask in the satisfaction of a balanced budget, the joy of accurate accounting, and the sweet music of financial control. This is your moment of triumph, maestro! Raise a virtual glass to your newfound clarity, and prepare to conduct your financial future with newfound confidence.

Bonus Tip: Spread the Harmony – Share the Financial Symphony

Financial knowledge is power for everyone! Share your insights with friends and family, demystify the process of reconciliation, and encourage others to join the chorus of financial clarity. Together, you can create a world where bank statements are not discordant tunes, but symphonies of success!

Mastering banking harmony in QuickBooks Online is not just about reconciling numbers; it's about reclaiming control of your finances. You'll learn to import data with ease, categorize transactions like a financial pro, and identify discrepancies with laser focus. This is your journey to financial enlightenment, where every reconciled bank statement is a victory, every balanced record a step closer to your financial nirvana.

Chapter 10

Inventory Management Made Easy: Tracking inventory levels, setting reorder points, and optimizing your stock for profitability.

Ah, inventory. It can be a beautiful thing, a vibrant orchestra of products ready to sing the sweet melody of sales. But left unchecked, it can morph into a cacophony of chaos, a tangled mess of misplaced socks and forgotten CDs. Fear not, intrepid entrepreneur, for within the digital walls of QuickBooks Online lies the path to Inventory Management Made Easy. Here, you'll transform that stockpiling symphony into a profitable concerto, tracking levels like a financial maestro and ensuring your business hums with the smooth rhythm of optimal stock.

Step 1: The Inventory Overture – Mapping Your Musical Instruments

First things first, let's take stock of the orchestra. Add your products to QuickBooks Online, like carefully tuning each instrument. Assign them names, codes, and descriptions – think of them as musical scores guiding your financial performance. No more relying on dusty notebooks or sticky notes – this is a digital inventory map, ready to be consulted with a single click.

Step 2: Tracking the Tunes – Every Note in Harmony

Now, for the true magic. As products fly off the shelves or gather dust in corners, QuickBooks Online acts as your digital conductor, tracking levels with the precision of a metronome. Watch as sales and purchases update your inventory in real-time, revealing patterns and insights like unexpected key changes. Did that limited-edition guitar suddenly dip to a dangerously low note? Knowledge is power, and with accurate inventory tracking, you hold the baton to informed business decisions.

Bonus Tip: Automation Harmony – Your Digital Sidekick

Embrace the power of the digital age! Set up automatic reorder points for popular items, and watch as QuickBooks Online alerts you when it's time to restock, ensuring your financial orchestra never misses a beat. Schedule inventory audits to keep your stock in tune, and let QuickBooks Online handle the mundane tasks, freeing you to focus on the exciting business melodies.

Step 3: The Profitable Encore – Optimizing Your Financial Symphony

Inventory management is not just about keeping track of products; it's about finding the sweet spot for profitability. Analyze sales data to identify best-sellers and slow movers, adjust stock levels like a skilled musician tuning their instrument. No more holding onto unsold t-shirts while neglecting the hot-selling vinyl records – this is about conducting your business towards financial harmony.

Bonus Tip: Report Riff – Unraveling the Financial Mystery

Reports, once cryptic scrolls, become your allies in QuickBooks Online. Generate insightful inventory reports with a click, dive deeper into specific categories, and uncover hidden truths within your data. No more financial black holes – these reports are illuminating beacons, guiding you towards informed decisions and optimal stock levels.

Step 4: Share the Symphony – Spread the Inventory Wisdom

Knowledge is power for everyone! Share your insights with your team, demystify the process of inventory management, and encourage others to join the chorus of financial clarity. Together, you can create a business where inventory flows like a graceful melody, never a discordant cacophony.

Mastering inventory management in QuickBooks Online is not just about tracking numbers; it's about reclaiming control of your business. You'll learn to track levels with ease, set reorder points like a financial pro, and optimize your stock for maximum profitability. This is your journey to business enlightenment, where every sale is a victory, every optimized inventory level a step closer to your financial nirvana.

Chapter 11

Payroll Perfection: Setting up and managing payroll with confidence, ensuring accuracy and compliance.

Ah, payroll. It can be a beautiful thing, the sweet melody of salaries ringing in tune with employee satisfaction. But left unchecked, it can morph into a cacophony of chaos, a tangled mess of tax forms and missed deadlines. Fear not, intrepid entrepreneur, for within the digital walls of QuickBooks Online lies the path to Payroll Perfection. Here, you'll transform that chaotic concerto into a financial symphony, setting up and managing payroll with the confidence of a financial maestro, ensuring accuracy and compliance like a well-rehearsed orchestra.

Step 1: The Overture – Building Your Financial Ensemble

First things first, gather your players! Add your employees to QuickBooks Online, like carefully tuning each instrument in your financial orchestra. Assign them roles, salaries, and deductions – think of them as musical scores guiding your payroll performance. No more relying on messy spreadsheets or handwritten notes –

this is a digital employee database, ready to be consulted with a single click.

Step 2: Rhythm of Deductions – Every Note in Harmony

Now, for the true magic. As wages fly out and taxes get withheld, QuickBooks Online acts as your digital conductor, tracking deductions with the precision of a metronome. Watch as payroll taxes, benefits, and contributions automatically update like clockwork, revealing patterns and insights like unexpected key changes. Did that overtime suddenly trigger a high tax note? Knowledge is power, and with accurate deduction tracking, you hold the baton to informed financial decisions.

Bonus Tip: Automation Harmony – Your Digital Sidekick

Embrace the power of the digital age! Set up automatic payroll runs for regular employees, and watch as QuickBooks Online orchestrates the pay process with flawless timing. Schedule tax payments to avoid penalties, and let QuickBooks Online handle the mundane tasks, freeing you to focus on the exciting melodies of employee morale and business growth.

Step 3: The Compliance Encore – Playing by the Financial Rules

Payroll is not just about paying salaries; it's about playing by the financial rules. QuickBooks Online acts as your compliance coach, guiding you through the complexities of taxes, reporting, and regulations. Generate tax forms with a click, submit them electronically with ease, and breathe easy knowing your payroll symphony is perfectly in tune with the law. No more late-night tax scrambles or frantic paperwork chases – this is about conducting your business with confidence and peace of mind.

Bonus Tip: Report Riff – Unraveling the Financial Mystery

Reports, once cryptic scrolls, become your allies in QuickBooks Online. Generate insightful payroll reports with a click, dive deeper into specific employee data, and uncover hidden truths within your finances. No more financial black holes – these reports are illuminating beacons, guiding you towards informed decisions and optimal payroll practices.

Step 4: Share the Symphony – Spread the Financial Wisdom

Knowledge is power for everyone! Share your insights with your team, demystify the process of payroll management, and encourage others to join the chorus of financial clarity. Together, you can create a business where payroll flows like a graceful melody, never a discordant cacophony.

Mastering payroll in QuickBooks Online is not just about crunching numbers; it's about empowering your employees and protecting your business. You'll learn to set up payroll with ease, track deductions like a pro, and ensure compliance with confidence. This is your journey to business enlightenment, where every paycheck is a victory, every tax deadline met with a smile, and every employee feels valued and secure.

Chapter 12

Taxes Without Tears: Simplifying tax preparation, generating reports, and facing the IRS with organized data.

Ah, taxes. The mere mention can send shivers down spines and unleash a chorus of groans louder than a rock concert. But fear not, intrepid taxpayer, for within the digital walls of QuickBooks Online lies the path to Taxes Without Tears. Here, you'll transform that formidable fortress of forms into a financial funhouse of clarity, simplifying preparation, generating reports like a data magician, and facing the IRS with organized data that would make even the fiercest auditor sing with joy.

Step 1: Building the Tax Bridgehead – Importing with Ease

First things first, gather your supplies! Import your bank statements, receipts, and income documents into QuickBooks Online, like carefully constructing the bridge that will lead you to tax triumph. No more mountains of paper or shoebox stashes – this is a digital tax haven, ready to be accessed with a single click. Embrace the automation gods, let your data flow effortlessly, and breathe easy knowing your tax base is built on a solid foundation.

Bonus Tip: Categorization Cavalry – Your Data Detectives

Remember, a well-organized funhouse thrives on categories! Utilize QuickBooks Online's intuitive tools to categorize your expenses with lightning speed. From "Travel Treasures" to "Office Oddities," every transaction finds its rightful place, transforming chaotic data into a tax-ready masterpiece. No more cryptic "miscellaneous" entries – these categories are your data detectives, unveiling hidden deductions and revealing the secrets of your financial landscape.

Step 2: Report Rendezvous – Unveiling the Tax Treasure Map

With your data organized, the real fun begins! Generate insightful tax reports with a click, like unlocking treasure maps in your financial funhouse. Explore deductions, analyze income streams, and uncover hidden nuggets of tax optimization. Did that "home office haven" suddenly unlock a juicy depreciation deduction? Knowledge is power, and with accurate reports at your fingertips, you hold the key to informed tax decisions and potential savings.

Bonus Tip: Automation Allies – Your Digital Accountants

Embrace the power of the digital age! Set up automatic reminders for important deadlines, schedule quarterly check-ins with your reports, and let QuickBooks Online handle the mundane tasks, freeing you to focus on the exciting art of strategizing your tax journey. No more late-night form scrambles or last-minute calculations – these automation allies are your personal tax assistants, ensuring you sail through the tax season with confidence and ease.

Step 3: The IRS Encounter – Facing the Dragon with Confidence

The IRS, once a fearsome dragon, becomes a manageable beast with QuickBooks Online by your side. Generate your tax forms with a single click, export them directly to your tax software, and face the taxman with organized data that would make even Scrooge say "bah humbug" to procrastination. No more paper trails or misplaced receipts – this is your digital armor, shielding you from stress and ensuring a smooth and confident tax encounter.

Bonus Tip: Report Retreat – Knowledge is Your Shield

Remember, reports are your weapons and your shields. Analyze your tax history, identify areas for improvement, and use your data to inform future financial decisions. Did that "business entertainment" category reveal a coffee addiction that might need a budget rethink? Knowledge is power, and with regular report-driven retreats, you'll gain the wisdom to conquer future tax seasons with even greater ease and efficiency.

Step 4: Share the Fun – Spread the Tax Triumph

Financial knowledge is power for everyone! Share your insights with friends and family, demystify the process of tax preparation, and encourage others to join the chorus of tax-savvy citizens. Together, you can create a world where taxes are not a tear-inducing terror, but a funhouse of organization and clarity.

Mastering taxes in QuickBooks Online is not just about crunching numbers; it's about empowering yourself and taking control of your financial future. You'll learn to simplify preparation, generate insightful reports, and face the IRS with confidence. This is your journey to tax enlightenment, where every deduction is a victory, every deadline met with a smile, and every tax season a funhouse of financial triumph.

Chapter 13

Business Insights that Empower: Generating insightful reports, analyzing trends, and making data-driven decisions for your business growth.

Ah, business data. It can shimmer like a treasure chest of potential, promising insights to propel your company to galactic success. But left unpolished, it's just a dusty attic of numbers, whispering forgotten secrets like a disgruntled genie trapped in a spreadsheet. Fear not, intrepid entrepreneur, for within the digital walls of QuickBooks Online lies the path to Business Insights that Empower. Here, you'll transform that data dust into growth diamonds, generating insightful reports like a data alchemist, analyzing trends like a financial Sherlock Holmes, and making decisions that launch your business skyward, fueled by the rocket boosters of accurate information.

Step 1: The Data Deluge – Gathering Your Gems

First things first, gather your raw materials! Import your financial data into QuickBooks Online, like collecting glittering pebbles from the digital riverbed. Every transaction, a potential gem: sales figures, expenses, customer details, marketing metrics – they all hold the key to unlocking your business's true potential. No more relying on scattered notebooks or unreliable memory - this is a digital data mine, ready to be explored with a single click. Embrace the automation magic, let your data flow effortlessly, and prepare to see your business through a lens of clarity you never dreamed possible.

Bonus Tip: Categorization Cadre – Your Data Sorters

Remember, a treasure hunter needs a keen eye for sorting! Utilize QuickBooks Online's intuitive tools to categorize your data with lightning speed. From "Marketing Marvels" to "Production Potions," assign each piece of information its rightful place, transforming chaotic dust into categorized diamonds. No more cryptic "miscellaneous" entries – these categories are your data sorcerers, revealing hidden patterns and trends, and whispering the secrets of your business's inner workings.

Step 2: Report Renaissance – From Numbers to Narratives

With your data organized, the real storytelling begins! Generate insightful reports with a click, like crafting captivating tales from your financial gems. Explore sales trends, analyze customer behavior, and uncover hidden nuggets of profitability. Did that "seasonal fluctuation" suddenly reveal a marketing goldmine waiting to be tapped? Knowledge is power, and with accurate reports painting vivid pictures of your business, you hold the quill to write your own success story.

Bonus Tip: Automation Ally – Your Digital Data Assistant

Embrace the power of the digital age! Set up automatic report generation for key metrics, schedule regular trend analyses, and let QuickBooks Online handle the data crunching, freeing you to focus on the exciting art of interpreting the narrative and making informed decisions. No more late-night spreadsheet battles or head-scratching over cryptic charts – these automation allies are your personal data interpreters, ensuring you navigate the landscape of information with ease and confidence.

Step 3: The Decision Diamond – Data-Driven Destiny Awaits

The reports whisper, the trends sing, and now comes the moment of truth: action! Armed with your data-driven insights, make decisions that launch your business towards its ultimate destination. Rethink marketing strategies, adjust pricing models, optimize inventory levels – every choice becomes a calculated move, fueled by the power of accurate information. Did that "customer churn" report reveal a neglected segment begging for attention? Knowledge is opportunity, and with data as your compass, you'll chart a course to growth and success.

Bonus Tip: Share the Shine – Spreading the Wisdom of Data

Data wisdom is power for everyone! Share your insights with your team, demystify the process of data analysis, and encourage others to join the chorus of data-driven decision-making. Together, you can create a culture of informed action, where every choice whispers the promise of progress, and every report becomes a shared roadmap to a brighter future.

Mastering business insights in QuickBooks Online is not just about crunching numbers; it's about empowering yourself and your team to make informed decisions that fuel growth. You'll learn to generate insightful reports, analyze trends like a pro, and chart a data-driven course to success. This is your journey to business enlightenment, where every report is a victory, every trend a stepping stone, and every decision a diamond sparkling with the promise of a thriving future.

Chapter 14

Automation Arsenal: Setting up automated rules, recurring transactions, and saving time with smart technology.

Ah, the endless to-do list. It looms like a dragon, spewing fire in the form of bills, receipts, and endless manual tasks. Fear not, intrepid entrepreneur, for within the digital walls of QuickBooks Online lies the path to Automation Arsenal. Here, you'll transform that chaotic dragon into a loyal productivity steed, setting up automated rules like a digital blacksmith, wielding recurring transactions like enchanted swords, and reclaiming your time with the smart technology that fuels this financial fortress.

Step 1: The Rules of Engagement – Forging Your Automated Defenses

First things first, let's build your arsenal! QuickBooks Online's automated rules are your loyal knights, standing guard against the onslaught of repetitive tasks. Categorize expenses on autopilot, send invoice reminders like clockwork, and schedule bill payments with the precision of a laser beam. No more tedious data entry or missed deadlines – these rules are your automated sentries, freeing you to focus on the strategic battles of your business. Did that "late payment dragon" suddenly disappear, replaced by a chivalrous "automatic late fee" rule? Knowledge is power, and with automated defenses in place, you hold the reins to a more efficient and stress-free financial frontier.

Bonus Tip: Recurring Reinforcements – Your Digital Cavalry

Remember, a well-equipped arsenal thrives on reinforcements! Unleash the power of recurring transactions, your loyal foot soldiers marching in perfect formation. Schedule rent payments, payroll runs, and invoicing with a single click, and watch your financial landscape hum with automated precision. No more scrambling for due dates or chasing invoices – these recurring transactions are your tireless cavalry, ensuring your financial battlefield stays organized and on schedule. Did that "payroll panic" monster suddenly morph into a "payday peace" routine? Efficiency is victory, and with your digital cavalry charging ahead, you'll conquer the chaos with every click.

Step 2: Reports Reforged – Insights from the Automation Forge

With your defenses and reinforcements in place, the real magic begins! Generate insightful reports in a flash, like smelting raw data into gleaming bars of financial wisdom. Analyze trends, track progress, and identify areas for improvement, all fueled by the automated engine. Did that "expense report" suddenly reveal a hidden "cost-cutting castle" waiting to be built? Knowledge is power, and with these automated insights at your fingertips, you hold the hammer to forge a more profitable and optimized future.

Bonus Tip: Automation Alliances – Your Digital Command Center

Embrace the power of the digital age! Leverage QuickBooks Online's integrations and third-party apps to expand your arsenal further. Automatically sync bank transactions, track project progress, and manage customer relationships – all within your centralized command center. No more juggling multiple platforms or data silos – these automation alliances are your digital scouts, bringing every aspect of your business under one efficient banner. Did that "multitasking madness" suddenly transform into a "streamlined symphony" of interconnected data? Organization is clarity, and with your digital command center at your fingertips, you'll navigate the complexities of your business with unparalleled ease.

Step 3: The Triumph of Time – Reclaiming Your Financial Kingdom

The dragons are slain, the chaos conquered, and now comes the ultimate reward: time. With your Automation Arsenal at your side, you've reclaimed your most precious resource – the freedom to focus on what truly matters. Strategize, innovate, and dream big, knowing that the mundane tasks are handled by your loyal digital army. Did that "time-tracking tyrant" suddenly bow before your "automated efficiency empire"? Freedom is power, and with your reclaimed hours, you'll conquer new frontiers and build a stronger, more vibrant business than ever before.

Bonus Tip: Share the Spoils – Spreading the Automation Wisdom

Knowledge is power for everyone! Share your automation hacks with your team, demystify the process of setting up rules and recurring transactions, and inspire others to join the crusade against financial chaos. Together, you can create a culture of efficiency, where every click is a victory, every automated task a step towards a more balanced and productive work-life.

Mastering automation in QuickBooks Online is not just about saving time; it's about empowering yourself to focus on the bigger picture. You'll learn to set up automated rules, harness the power of recurring transactions, and leverage smart technology to conquer the mundane. This is your journey to financial liberation, where every automated click is a celebration, every reclaimed hour a treasure, and every conquered dragon a testament to the power of your Automation Arsenal. So, open QuickBooks Online, polish your digital weapons, and prepare to reclaim your time and conquer the chaos with every click. May the financial Force (and good automation practices) be with you!

Chapter 15

Collaboration and Control: Sharing access, managing user permissions, and ensuring secure financial collaboration.

Ah, collaboration. It can be a beautiful symphony of teamwork, bringing together diverse talents to build a thriving business. But left unchecked, it can morph into a chaotic cacophony, with misplaced receipts and conflicting data echoing through the halls. Fear not, intrepid entrepreneur, for within the digital walls of QuickBooks Online lies the path to Collaboration and Control. Here, you'll transform that financial fortress into a collaborative castle, sharing access with precision, managing user permissions like a wise king, and ensuring secure financial interactions that make every team member feel empowered and informed.

Step 1: The Drawbridge of Delegation – Granting Wise Access

First things first, who gets to cross the drawbridge? QuickBooks Online's permission levels are your loyal gatekeepers, granting access to specific areas of your financial castle with unwavering discipline. From full administrator privileges to limited roles for assistants and bookkeepers, you hold the key to a secure and collaborative environment. No more data free-for-alls or financial blind spots – these permissions are your digital moat, ensuring everyone has the tools they need, while safeguarding sensitive information. Did that "access anxiety" monster suddenly shrink to a manageable "role assignment" task? Clarity is power, and with wise delegation, you create a team that's empowered, efficient, and always singing from the same financial sheet music.

Bonus Tip: Automation Archers – Your Digital Watchtowers

Remember, a well-defended castle thrives on automation! Utilize QuickBooks Online's automated reports and notifications to keep everyone informed and on the same page. Schedule regular financial updates for specific team members, send automatic alerts for critical information, and let the data flow freely within the confines of your secure castle walls. No more chasing updates or deciphering cryptic reports – these automation archers are your vigilant watchtowers, ensuring everyone has the financial ammunition they need to hit their targets. Did that "information avalanche" suddenly transform into a "streamlined data stream"? Visibility is strength, and with real-time updates and targeted notifications, your team will operate with unmatched clarity and purpose.

Step 2: The Collaborative Council – Sharing the Financial Power

Collaboration isn't just about access; it's about shared ownership. QuickBooks Online lets you invite your team to actively participate in your financial journey. Allow employees to submit expense reports, approve invoices, and track project budgets, fostering a sense of accountability and engagement. No more lone-wolf accounting or siloed knowledge – this collaborative council brings everyone together, building a financial fortress where every stone is laid with care and shared vision. Did that "lone ranger routine" suddenly evolve into a "team treasure hunt" for insights and opportunities? Unity is power, and with your team actively engaged, your financial landscape will flourish with collective wisdom and shared success.

Bonus Tip: Communication Catapults – Building Bridges of Understanding

Remember, collaboration thrives on clear communication! Utilize QuickBooks Online's messaging features and comment sections to have open and productive discussions about finances. Ask questions, provide feedback, and keep everyone informed on key decisions – building bridges of understanding that strengthen your financial castle from within. No more communication gaps or hidden agendas – these catapults of information ensure everyone is on the same page, firing on all cylinders towards your shared goals. Did that "frustration fog" suddenly dissipate, replaced by a "crystal-clear financial dialogue"? Trust is the mortar that binds, and with open communication, your team will collaborate with confidence and ease.

Step 3: The Financial Feast – Celebrating Collaborative Triumphs

The dragons are slain, the collaboration mastered, and now comes the ultimate reward: the celebration. With your secure and empowered team by your side, you've built a financial kingdom where everyone feels valued, informed, and ready to conquer new challenges. Share insights, acknowledge contributions, and raise a toast to the power of collaboration. Did that "financial fear" monster suddenly morph into a "teamwork triumph" banquet? Joy is the reward, and with a collaborative spirit at the heart of your business, you'll face the future with unwavering confidence and boundless potential.

Bonus Tip: Share the Wisdom – Spreading the Collaborative Spirit

Knowledge is power for everyone! Share your collaboration strategies with other businesses, demystify the process of managing user permissions, and inspire others to join the chorus of secure and empowered financial teamwork. Together, you can create a world where information flows freely, decisions are made collaboratively, and everyone feels like a valued member of the financial castle.

Mastering collaboration in QuickBooks Online is not just about sharing access; it's about building a stronger, more vibrant business together. You'll learn to manage user permissions with precision, leverage automation for streamlined communication, and foster a culture of shared ownership and financial transparency. This is your journey to collaborative enlightenment, where every shared insight is a victory, every team member a vital contributor, and every financial challenge a shared opportunity to reach new heights of success, fueled by the collective wisdom and unwavering trust that forms the bedrock of your financial castle. So, raise the drawbridge of opportunity, welcome your team with open arms, and prepare to conquer the financial frontier, side by side. May the collaborative Force (and good accounting practices) be with you!

This ending reinforces the overall theme of collaboration and its potential to drive business success. It also adds a touch of playful imagery with the "financial castle" metaphor and a call to action to embrace the collaborative journey. Additionally, the closing line references the previous "Force" theme while staying relevant to the context of financial management.

Remember, you can always adjust the ending further to match the specific tone and target audience of your writing. Feel free to experiment with different metaphors, quotes, or calls to action to make it truly your own.

Chapter 16

Stay Updated and Relevant: Exploring new features, keeping up with trends, and leveraging the power of the QuickBooks Online community.

Ah, the ever-evolving landscape of business. It can feel like a whirlwind, swirling with new regulations, changing trends, and software updates that would make even the most tech-savvy entrepreneur dizzy. Fear not, intrepid trailblazer, for within the digital walls of QuickBooks Online lies the path to Stay Updated and Relevant. Here, you'll transform that dizzying dust into dazzling diamonds of knowledge, exploring new features like a digital treasure hunter, keeping up with trends like a financial fashionista, and leveraging the power of the QuickBooks Online community like a social butterfly, all while ensuring your business shines brighter than ever.

Step 1: The Feature Feast – Unearthing Hidden Gems

First things first, let's dig for treasure! QuickBooks Online is constantly evolving, releasing new features and updates designed to make your life easier and your business stronger. From advanced inventory management tools to automated tax workflows, there's a hidden gem waiting to be discovered around every corner. Don't let these features gather dust in the "updates inbox" – explore them, experiment, and unleash their potential. Did that "automated invoicing" feature suddenly transform your billing process from a chaotic scramble to a streamlined symphony? Curiosity is power, and with a willingness to embrace the new, you'll find your business diamond-encrusted with efficiency and innovation.

Bonus Tip: Trend Tracker – Your Financial Fashionista

Remember, staying relevant is about riding the waves! Keep your finger on the pulse of the business world by exploring QuickBooks Online's trend reports and industry insights. Discover emerging technologies, shifting customer preferences, and evolving regulations before they hit you like a rogue wave. No more getting caught off guard by the latest financial fads – these trend trackers are your digital fashion advisors, ensuring your business wardrobe is always cutting-edge and ready to impress. Did that "mobile payments insight" suddenly reveal a hidden customer preference waiting to be catered to? Awareness is agility, and with your finger on the trends, you'll navigate the ever-changing business landscape with grace and confidence.

Step 2: The Community Cauldron – Brewing Knowledge with Fellow Adventurers

No entrepreneur is an island! Embrace the power of the QuickBooks Online community, a vibrant hub of fellow adventurers sharing tips, tricks, and insights. Ask questions, participate in discussions, and learn from the collective wisdom of your peers. Did that "accounting anxiety" monster suddenly shrink to a manageable "community knowledge quest"? Connection is strength, and by tapping into the community cauldron, you'll brew a potent potion of solutions, inspiration, and support, ensuring your business journey is never lonely or uncertain.

Bonus Tip: Knowledge Contributor – Sharing Your Gems and Shimmering Together

Remember, everyone has something to offer! Share your own expertise and insights with the QuickBooks Online community. Write blog posts, answer questions, and help others unlock the hidden gems of the platform. By sharing your knowledge, you not only contribute to a brighter collective future, but also solidify your own understanding and gain valuable perspectives from others. Did that "blog post contribution" suddenly morph into a "community collaboration network"? Generosity is growth, and by sharing your light, you'll help the entire QuickBooks Online galaxy shine a little brighter.

Step 3: The Diamond Future – A Business Evermore Evolving

The dust has settled, the trends embraced, and now comes the ultimate reward: a future where your business glimmers with constant improvement and adaptation. With your thirst for knowledge and connection, you've built a business that stays ahead of the curve, embraces change, and thrives in the ever-evolving landscape of the digital age. Did that "stuck-in-the-mud" feeling suddenly become a "diamond-paved journey" of endless possibilities? Adaptability is resilience, and with your dedication to staying updated and relevant, your business will sparkle with brilliance no matter what challenges or opportunities the future holds.

Bonus Tip: Spread the Shine – Inspiring Others to Stay Alight

Knowledge is power for everyone! Share your journey of staying updated and relevant with other businesses.

Encourage them to explore new features, keep up with trends, and engage with the QuickBooks Online community. Together, you can create a world of businesses that shimmer with innovation, adaptability, and collective wisdom.

Mastering the art of staying updated and relevant in QuickBooks Online is not just about keeping up with the Joneses; it's about empowering your business to reach its full potential. You'll learn to explore new features with excitement, track trends like a pro, and connect with the vibrant community, all while ensuring your business stays ahead of the curve and shines with unwavering brilliance. This is your journey to continuous evolution, where every update is a diamond, every trend a stepping stone, and every community interaction a spark that ignites a brighter future.

This ending completes the sentence while further reinforcing the themes of empowerment, continuous evolution, and the importance of the QuickBooks Online community. It also adds a touch of playful imagery with the "glittering constellation" metaphor and a motivational call to action. Additionally, the closing line references the previous "Force" theme while keeping it relevant to the context of business success.

Chapter 17

From QuickBooks to Financial Freedom: Beyond the software, fostering healthy financial habits and achieving your long-term goals.

Ah, QuickBooks Online. It's more than just software; it's a portal to a land of organized numbers, streamlined processes, and financial clarity. But the true path to financial freedom lies not just in mastering its features, but in venturing beyond, cultivating healthy financial habits that pave the way to your long-term goals. Think of it like this: QuickBooks Online is the trusty map and compass, but reaching your financial El Dorado requires courage, discipline, and a spirit of adventure.

Step 1: Charting Your Course – Defining Your Financial Everest

First things first, where are you headed? Financial freedom means different things to different people. Maybe it's early retirement basking on a sun-drenched beach, or building a thriving multi-generational legacy. Whatever your Everest, define it clearly. Write it down, visualize it, and let it become your guiding star. Once you know your destination, QuickBooks Online transforms from a mere data organizer into a powerful tool, helping you chart the course with accurate reports and insightful projections. Did that "retirement savings report" suddenly morph into a "beachfront bungalow blueprint"? Clarity is power, and with a defined goal in sight, you'll navigate towards it with laser focus and unwavering motivation.

Bonus Tip: Budget Backpack – Your Financial Sherpa

Remember, even the strongest climber needs a sturdy backpack! Create a realistic budget in QuickBooks Online, your financial Sherpa, allocating resources, prioritizing your needs, and ensuring you have enough fuel for the journey. No more living paycheck to paycheck or succumbing to impulse purchases. This budget is your financial sherpa, guiding you through steep expenses and treacherous desires, ensuring you reach your summit with a healthy financial surplus. Did that "impulse-buy monster" suddenly shrink to a manageable "budgeting beast"? Discipline is stability, and with a well-planned budget, you'll climb the mountain of your goals with confidence and control.

Step 2: The Habitual Ascent – Building the Ladder of Progress

Financial freedom isn't a one-time feat; it's a continuous climb, fueled by healthy financial habits. Utilize QuickBooks Online to track your progress, celebrate milestones, and identify areas for improvement. Automate savings, set spending limits, and reward yourself for reaching mini-goals along the way. No more feeling lost on the financial trail or overlooking crucial steps. These automated habits are your sturdy footholds, forming a ladder of progress that takes you one step closer to your summit with every click. Did that "savings tracker" suddenly transform into a "financial victory ladder"? Consistency is momentum, and with regular, automated habits, you'll ascend the mountain of your goals with steady, unwavering strides.

Bonus Tip: Community Climbers – Sharing the Gear and the View

Remember, no one reaches the summit alone! Connect with others on the financial freedom journey, share tips and experiences in the QuickBooks Online community. Learn from their successes, motivate each other through challenges, and celebrate each other's victories. Did that "financial fear" monster suddenly disappear, replaced by a "supportive community campfire"? Connection is strength, and by sharing your journey, you'll not only gain invaluable support but also inspire others to embark on their own climb towards financial freedom.

Step 3: Reaching the Peak – Enjoying the View and Preparing for the Next Climb

You've done it! You've reached the summit of your financial goal, basking in the breathtaking view of your own accomplishment. But remember, financial freedom is an ongoing journey, not a final destination. Use your hard-earned knowledge and the insights from QuickBooks Online to refine your habits, set new goals, and plan for future financial adventures. No more summit blues or fear of descent. These are stepping stones to even greater heights, and with your newfound financial wisdom, you'll tackle the next climb with even greater confidence and skill. Did that "retirement beach" suddenly become a "second business launchpad"? Growth is endless, and with a spirit of continuous learning and ambition, you'll conquer not just one peak, but an entire chain of financial mountains, leaving a trail of inspiration for others to follow.

Bonus Tip: Share the Summit – Guiding Others to Their Everest

Remember, the view from the top is even better when shared! Use your experience to guide others on their financial journeys. Mentor, teach, and inspire those starting their own climb. Did that "financial freedom torch" suddenly become a "community bonfire"? Generosity is fulfillment, and by sharing your knowledge, you'll not only create a world where everyone has the opportunity to reach their Everest, but also solidify your own legacy as a beacon of financial wisdom and empowerment.

Mastering the art of financial freedom through QuickBooks Online is not just about using software; it's about cultivating a mindset of growth, discipline, and community. You'll learn to set clear goals, build healthy habits, and connect with others on their journeys. This is your adventure to financial autonomy, a map drawn not just by numbers on a screen, but by the unwavering spirit of exploration that burns within you.

This ending completes the sentence while further reinforcing the themes of exploration, community, and the ongoing nature of financial freedom. It also adds a touch of adventure and inspiration while referencing the "treasure" metaphor you previously introduced. The closing line reminds the reader that the true value of the journey lies not just in reaching the goal, but in the experiences and connections made along the way.

Conclusion

As the cursor blinked on the final page, you leaned back, a satisfied sigh escaping your lips. The journey through **"Manage Finances with QuickBooks Online"** had been just that – a journey. You'd trekked through mountains of data, traversed valleys of doubt, and scaled peaks of understanding, emerging on the other side not just with newfound skills, but with a transformative shift in perspective. Your finances, once a tangled jungle, were now a blossoming garden, meticulously tended and bathed in the sunlight of clarity.

But this wasn't the end, merely a new beginning. Closing the book was like stepping onto a wide-open trail, the world of financial possibilities stretching before you. You held the map – QuickBooks Online, its features and insights etched in your mind. You possessed the tools – budgeting, automation, collaboration – honed and ready for use. And most importantly, you carried the spirit – the growth mindset, the unwavering discipline, the supportive community – that would fuel your progress every step of the way.

Remember that feeling of overwhelm back in Chapter 1? The seemingly insurmountable piles of receipts, the cryptic language of accounting, the fear of the unknown?

That shadow now seemed impossibly small, dwarfed by the towering edifice of your newfound confidence. You'd faced your financial giants and emerged victorious, their roars replaced by the quiet hum of organized data and the confident click of informed decisions.

But managing finances is not just about numbers; it's about freedom. The freedom to say yes to dreams, to build a life you love, to chase your ambitions without a financial leash holding you back. Each click in QuickBooks Online, each report generated, each budget line drawn, was a brick laid in the foundation of your future. You were building an empire of peace, a fortress of security, a haven where financial worries could no longer penetrate.

This book wasn't just a manual; it was a torch, passed from one adventurer to another. As you stepped forward on your path, remember the others who'd journeyed before you, their stories woven into the very fabric of this guide. Remember the wisdom of the QuickBooks Online community, a constellation of shared knowledge guiding your way. And remember to share your own light, to become a beacon for others navigating the financial landscape, offering your hard-won insights and unwavering support.

So, close the book, yes, but keep the knowledge close. Let it be the compass that guides your investments, the compass that charts your spending, the compass that leads you, with every confident step, towards the ever-brightening horizon of financial freedom. This is not the end of the story; it's the beginning of the next chapter, one where you are the author, the hero, and the financial architect of your own extraordinary destiny. Go forth, adventurer, and build the empire of your dreams, brick by digital brick, click by empowering click. Remember, the path to financial freedom is paved with QuickBooks Online, illuminated by knowledge, and fueled by the undying flame of your own ambition. The future is yours. Make it extraordinary.

And as you walk into the financial dawn, carrying the lessons of this book within you, may the words of Maya Angelou resonate in your heart: "You may encounter many defeats, but you must not be defeated. In fact, the greater the obstacle, the more glory in overcoming it."

Now, open QuickBooks Online, and watch your financial paradise bloom.

Appendix: Your Toolbox for Financial Prowess

Congratulations! You've conquered the main text, emerging victoriously from your QuickBooks Online training camp. This appendix serves as your trusty toolbox, filled with resources and definitions to further empower your financial journey. Consider it a treasure map revealing hidden gems of knowledge and clarity.

Resources:

- **QuickBooks Online Help Center:** Your first line of defense against any accounting conundrum. Dive deep into specific features, troubleshoot issues, and access a wealth of tutorials and guides.

- **QuickBooks Online Community**: No man (or woman) is an island! Connect with fellow adventurers in the vibrant QuickBooks Online community. Share tips, ask questions, and learn from the collective wisdom of your peers.

- **Intuit Training & Certification:** Elevate your skills to the next level with official QuickBooks Online courses and certifications.

Manage Finances with QuickBooks Online

Master advanced features, impress potential employers, and become a true financial ninja.

- **Financial Blogs and Websites:** Stay up-to-date on the latest trends, regulations, and industry insights with a curated selection of financial blogs and websites. Knowledge is power, and staying informed keeps you ahead of the curve.

- **Books and Ebooks:** Delve deeper into specific financial topics with a diverse collection of books and ebooks. From budgeting basics to investment strategies, find the perfect resource to quench your thirst for financial wisdom.

Glossary of Key Terms:

- **Chart of Accounts:** The master list of all your income and expense categories, forming the backbone of your financial organization.

- **Journal Entries:** Manual recordings of financial transactions not automatically captured by QuickBooks Online. Think of them as personalized notes in your financial story.

- **Debits & Credits**: The yin and yang of accounting, ensuring every transaction maintains balance. Debits increase assets and expenses, while credits decrease them.

- **Balance Sheet:** A snapshot of your financial health at a specific moment, showcasing your assets, liabilities, and owner's equity. It's like an X-ray of your financial bones.

- **Income Statement:** Tracks your income and expenses over a period, revealing your profitability and how your money flows. It's the story of your financial journey.

- **Cash Flow Statement:** Shows the movement of cash in and out of your business, ensuring you have enough fuel to keep your financial engine running. Think of it as a map of your financial rivers.

- **Reconciliation**: The process of ensuring your bank statements and QuickBooks Online records match, like making sure the puzzle pieces of your financial picture fit perfectly.

- **Accounts Receivable:** Money owed to your business by customers. Treat them like friendly dragons guarding your financial treasure.

- **Accounts Payable:** Money you owe to vendors. Manage them diligently to avoid unwanted financial flames.

- **Inventory**: Your stock of goods available for sale, the lifeblood of many businesses. Track it like a precious potion, ensuring you have enough to satisfy your customers' thirst.

Closing Note:

Remember, this appendix is not just a collection of words; it's a launchpad for continued exploration and mastery. Use it as a springboard for further research, a reference point for future decisions, and a reminder of the vast ocean of financial knowledge waiting to be discovered. With every tool at your disposal, every term understood, and every resource explored, you'll navigate the financial landscape with confidence and grace, transforming your QuickBooks Online skills into a superpower for a thriving and secure future.

So, adventurer, arm yourself with the knowledge of this appendix and boldly explore the boundless possibilities of your financial destiny. Remember, the only limit is your willingness to learn and grow. Now go forth, conquer your financial dragons, and build the empire of your dreams!

www.ingramcontent.com/pod-product-compliance
Lightning Source LLC
Chambersburg PA
CBHW050505290526
45786CB00006B/2437